Layla goes to *Ballet* class

Anne-Marie Pos-Terlouw

Illustrations by Luana Bran (Deveo Media)

For Emilia,
who discovered ballet.

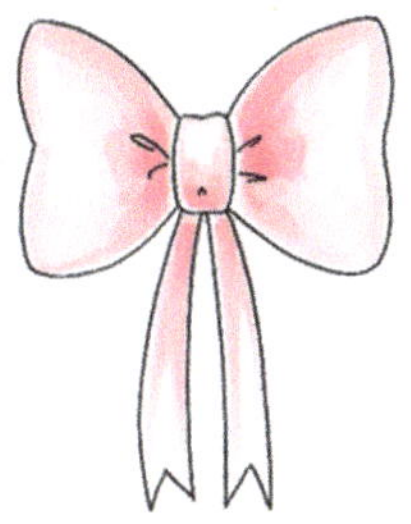

It is the weekend and Layla is allowed to watch a few videos before breakfast.
Mom puts some bread in the oven, and Dad is cooking eggs.

Mom calls out, "Layla, are you ready for breakfast?"

But she hears no response. Mom goes to check on Layla and finds her looking
at the screen intently.
On the screen, there is a beautiful ballerina.

"Oh mom, I want that too!"Layla says.

"Really? Would you like to do ballet, Layla?" Mom asks.
"Well, then we need to go and see if we can find ballet classes for you."

Mom puts down a plate with a sandwich for Layla."Now eat your breakfast, and we
will go to the supermarket together."

LIVE

There is music coming from the market square.

 Layla sees children dancing. They are wearing bright-colored clothing and are dancing together to the music. Layla recognizes it a little bit from the videos she has seen.

"Look Mom, they are doing ballet." Layla points out.

Mom spots an older girl in a purple T-shirt that says "Studio Dance". And she is holding something in her hands.

Mom walks toward her.

"Hello" says the girl.
"Would your little girl like to try ballet?"

"Yes, she would." Mom replies.

"Here you go,"says the girl. "This is a flyer
about our dance studio."

Mom takes it and puts it in her bag.
She will look at it and read it later at home.

"Would you like to meet miss Zoey?" the girl asks.
"She is over there." She points to a booth with dance pictures, posters and even a
real tutu.

Mom looks at Layla, "Shall we go up and see?"

"Yes," Layla replies.

Stud
D

As soon as they approach the booth,somebody walks over to meet them.

 "Hello, I am Miss Zoey, I am a dance teacher and owner of Studio Dance."

She smiles at Layla and says,"I bet you would like to try ballet, wouldn't you?"

Layla starts to blush and looks at Mom.

"Go ahead." Mom says encouragingly."Go ahead and tell Miss Zoey."

"Yes," Layla admits.

"I saw a video with a beautiful ballerina. I want to do that too!"

"Wonderful!" Miss Zoey says and claps her hands.

"I think we can arrange for you to come try real soon."

She looks at Mom. Mom nods her head.

"Yes, we can." she says.

"Can you come in on Thursday at four o'clock?"

 Miss Zoey asks.

"Yes, no problem." says mom.

Layla has a beaming smile on her face.

"Mom, how many nights will that be until Thursday?" Layla asks.

"Five, sweetie," Mom replies.

Layla jumps up. She can hardly wait.

"What does Layla have to wear to her first class?" Mom asks Miss Zoey.

"Leggings, a T-shirt and socks are fine for the first time. Let's first see if you like it. When you decide you love it, you can always buy the appropriate attire like a leotard and ballet shoes."

Mom nods her head and smiles to Miss Zoey.

 "Thank you, Miss Zoey. We will see you on Thursday!"

That night, Layla can hardly fall asleep. It is all so exciting and fun.

Five nights to go, and then she will go to ballet class!

The next days go by way too slowly for Layla.

Paying attention to do homework is also very difficult.

She can only think about ballet class. But she knows she has to be patient.

 It is almost Thursday!

At breakfast on Thursday morning, Layla can hardly eat.

It is so exciting! She bounces up and down in her chair with excitement.

“Are you looking forward to this afternoon?” asks Mom.

“Yes!” shouts Layla.

“Very good,” replies Mom. “Now go ahead and put on your shoes. I am taking you

to school, and I will see you this afternoon.”

That afternoon, Layla and Mom arrive at the dance studio. The dance studio is a special place. You can feel it when you walk in. It feels nice, cozy and warm.

There is already a ballet class in session. Layla can see the other girls in this class dancing. The girls are all wearing pink leotards and pink ballet shoes.
In their hair, they are wearing beautiful ribbons and colored pins.

And what a beautiful room. The floor is made of really nice, dark wood, and the walls are a warm purple tone. There are wooden sticks on the walls.
"Why are those there?" Layla asks herself .

Layla is already wearing her leggings and T-shirt.

She is all ready to enter the dance studio.

Just a little bit longer and this class will be ending.

 There are more children waiting in the hallway. Moms, dads and grandparents are also waiting outside; otherwise, it will be too busy inside.

Because it is Layla's first day today, Mom is allowed to walk her into the studio. The first time at a new place can be a little tense.

Then it's time! The dancers are coming out of the room. Their class has ended. Layla is really excited to enter the studio. Finally, she will be in a real ballet class.

And there is miss Zoey!"Hello Layla," she says.

"Lovely that you are here. Would you like to come and sit next to me today?

I will introduce you to the rest of the group."

That is indeed something Layla likes, and she quickly seats herself

next to Miss Zoey on the floor.

A girl with dark brown hair seats herself next to Layla.

"Hi, I am Mila." says the girl.

"I have been in ballet for a long time. You are new today."

Layla nods. " It is very fun here," Mila says.

Layla sees mom standing in the door opening.

Mom waves and says, "Have fun!"

Layla waves back and smiles at Mom.

Miss Zoey starts class:"Good afternoon, everybody.

This is Layla, today is her first class."

The other children look at her, immediately smile and wave at her.

"When you hear your name, please say you are here. And then you may tell a short story to us all," Miss Zoey says.

"We always do that at the beginning of class, Layla.

 Amaya, you may start today."

Amaya smiles and says, "Yes, Miss Zoey, I am here."

Amaya is wearing a beautiful, pink headscarf, which exactly matches her pink leotard. She says that her grandmother came to visit.

"I don't have a beautiful leotard." Layla says aloud.

"Oh, that's alright." Miss Zoey answers "None of us did when we started with ballet. It is perfectly alright to get a leotard and ballet shoes later."

Layla gets to know a few other children. Lilian, who has light, yellow hair. Nora with orange hair. And Jason, a little boy in ballet class. Getting to know them is so much fun. Layla did not know she could have so much fun in ballet class. This group looks a lot like her own class in school, with so many different children.

 Layla feels right at home.

"All right" Miss Zoey starts. "Let's get up and stand on our feet. We will start dancing all together in a circle."
Layla stands up, and Mila takes her hand.

Miss Zoey starts singing a song, and everybody twirls and jumps on their spot. Layla dances along and is having a great time. After this warming-up dance, they are going to dance at the ballet barre.

"What is this?" Layla asks.

Miss Zoey explains, "Those sticks on the walls, we call ballet barres. We stand next to the barre and lay one hand on it. Sometimes two hands.
The barre helps us practice ballet postures and movements without falling down.
We practice pliés, relevés and tendus. Those are knee bends, standing on your toes, and stretching and gliding your legs in and out.
All ballet steps have those three basic moves in them, so we must make sure we do them well.
You do that by practicing. A lot."

“But I don’t know how to do that.” Layla says.

“Don’t worry,” Miss Zoey answers. “I will help you. Look at me and try to do

 as I do as best as you can.”

Mila also wants to help Layla.

“Look, like this.” Mila says, and shows her.

Miss Zoey starts the music again, and they all dance beautiful ballet steps together.

Nora has some difficulties practicing on one spot.

And now she is hanging upside down on the barre.

Miss Zoey laughs. “Nora, what happened? You can’t do ballet like that!”

Nora smiles and turns upright. Now she will be able to do it.

“Good job, Nora. That looks good, everybody.” Miss Zoey says, complimenting

the whole class.

“We will do it again next week. And you will see it will become easier and easier

every week until you are really good at it” Miss Zoey smiles.

“We will keep practicing together.”

Layla nods.

Now they are going to dance across the whole room.

Miss Zoey puts down some rope on the floor.

Then she gently rises up on her toes and carefully walks along the rope.

She is holding her arms out at her sides to help her balance.

"Did you see how I did that?" she asks the children. "Now it's your turn to try.

Mila may go first, then Layla and then Amaya.

One by one, and one after the other, the ballet dancers walk along the rope.

And it's going really well.

"Good job, everybody!" says Miss Zoey.

Miss Zoey takes out a suitcase and opens it. In the suitcase there are beautifully,

colored butterfly wings. Miss Zoey takes one pair out, and calls out a name.

Then she gives the wings to that child.

Layla waits patiently until she hears her name. Then she receives her wings.

Wow, they are magnificent!The wings have two loops, one for each arm.

Layla sticks her arms through the loops, and now the wings are safely on her back.

Miss Zoey explains: "We are going to tippytoe, and here in the middle of the

room, we are going to fly just like butterflies."

Miss Zoey puts down a lovely, green scarf on the floor.

"This is what you may jump over."

She shows them how, just in case they aren't sure what to do.

"Oh!" Layla says to Mila "Miss Zoey can jump really high!"

She is excited to try it herself. Patiently she awaits her turn. Then she runs on her

toes, puts out her arms, and jumps high in the air over the green scarf.

"Nicely done, Layla!"miss Zoey calls out.

"Well done for your first time." She smiles.

After the butterfly dance, everybody returns the wings to miss Zoey.
She puts them back into the suitcase and puts it away for next time.
"Let's go sit down in a circle and sing our goodbye song."
"Oh, is class over already?"asks Layla. She had so much fun, she could have danced another hour.
"Yes, it's time." Miss Zoey says.
"Look, the next group is awaiting their own class."

"Did you have a good time today, Layla?" asks Miss Zoey.
Layla nods. She has a big smile on her face and rosy cheeks from dancing.

Mom is back in the hallway. Layla runs towards her.
"Mom, may I come to ballet class next week?" Layla asks.
"Sure, Layla," Mom says. "Come, let's go home so you can tell your Dad about your first ballet class."

Layla turns around and waves: "Bye Mila, bye Nora, bye Amaya and bye Jason. See you all next week!"

That night Layla sleeps like a baby.

In her dream she is dancing as a real ballerina in a beautiful garden.

She is wearing a magnificent, golden tutu and dances past pink roses

and yellow daffodils.

Mom comes in the bedroom to check if Layla is asleep.

She sees Layla sleeping with a big smile on her face.

"Is she dreaming about ballet ?" Mom wonders.

And next week, Layla will go to ballet class again.

Layla's ballet adventure with her new friends and ballet teacher has really begun!